# Painting With Transparency: The Art Of Watercolor Made Easy

Kristi Ryan

Published by Kristi Ryan, 2024.

# Table of Contents

# Introduction

Have you ever gazed at a watercolor painting and marveled at its ethereal beauty, wondering how artists achieve such luminous effects with seemingly effortless brushstrokes? Watercolor, with its delicate washes and transparent layers, has captivated artists and art lovers for centuries. It's a medium that dances on the edge between control and spontaneity, offering endless possibilities for creative expression. Whether you're a complete beginner or an experienced artist looking to explore new techniques, "The Art of Watercolor Made Easy" is your comprehensive guide to mastering this enchanting medium.

Watercolor painting has a rich history dating back to ancient times, with examples found in Egyptian papyrus paintings and early Renaissance works. However, it wasn't until the 18th and 19th centuries that watercolor truly came into its own as a respected artistic medium, championed by masters like J.M.W. Turner and John Singer Sargent. Today, watercolor continues to evolve, offering artists a unique blend of traditional techniques and contemporary innovations. What sets watercolor apart from other painting mediums is its inherent transparency and fluidity, allowing artists to create luminous effects and subtle gradations of color that are difficult to achieve with other paints. The unpredictable nature of water and pigment interactions also adds an element of spontaneity and surprise to the creative process, making each painting a thrilling adventure.

In "The Art of Watercolor Made Easy," we take a fresh approach to teaching this timeless medium. Unlike many traditional watercolor guides that focus solely on technique, this book offers a holistic view of watercolor painting, combining technical instruction with insights into the creative process and practical advice for developing your unique artistic voice. We believe that mastering watercolor is not just about learning brush techniques or color theory – it's about understanding the medium's inherent qualities and harnessing them to express your creative vision. Throughout the book, we'll explore how to embrace the fluid nature of watercolor, working with its transparency and unpredictability rather than fighting against them.

As we journey through the pages of this book, we'll explore several key themes and concepts that are essential to becoming a proficient and confident watercolor artist. First, we'll delve into the fundamental techniques that form the foundation of watercolor painting, including wet-on-wet and wet-on-dry methods, washes, glazes, and layering. Understanding these techniques will give you the tools to create a wide range of effects and textures in your paintings. Next, we'll focus on mastering transparency, one of the most captivating aspects of watercolor. You'll learn how to control water-to-paint ratios, build up layers for luminous effects, and preserve white space to create highlights and a sense of light in your work.

Composition and design play a crucial role in creating compelling watercolor paintings, and we'll explore these principles in depth. You'll discover how to use value and contrast effectively, plan and sketch your paintings, and create dynamic compositions that draw the viewer's eye. We'll also dive into specific subjects that are popular among watercolor artists, including landscapes, still lifes, florals, and portraits. Each of these subjects presents unique challenges and opportunities, and we'll provide step-by-step guidance on how to approach them with confidence.

For those looking to push their skills further, we'll explore advanced watercolor techniques such as negative painting, lifting, and the use of masking fluid. We'll also discuss how to incorporate mixed media elements into your watercolor paintings, opening up new avenues for experimentation and creative expression. Finally, we'll guide you through the process of developing your personal style, helping you find inspiration, experiment with different approaches, and continuously improve your craft.

"The Art of Watercolor Made Easy" is designed for a wide range of readers, from complete beginners who have never picked up a brush to intermediate artists looking to refine their skills and explore new techniques. Even experienced watercolorists will find valuable insights and fresh perspectives to enhance their practice. If you've always been curious about watercolor but felt intimidated by its reputation for being difficult to control, this book will show you how to embrace the medium's unique qualities and turn them to your advantage. For those who have some experience with watercolor but feel stuck in their progress, we'll provide the tools and inspiration to break through creative barriers and take your work to the next level.

By reading this book and following its guidance, you'll gain a comprehensive understanding of watercolor painting that goes beyond mere technique. You'll develop the skills to create luminous, expressive paintings that capture the essence of your subjects and reflect your unique artistic vision. More than just a set of instructions, this book will help you cultivate a mindset that allows you to approach watercolor with confidence and joy, embracing both the challenges and the delightful surprises that come with working in this medium.

You'll learn how to see the world through a watercolorist's eyes, noticing the play of light and shadow, the subtle variations in color, and the textures and patterns that can be translated into paint. As you progress through the book, you'll discover how to use watercolor to express not just what you see, but what you feel about your subject. Whether you're painting a sun-drenched landscape, a delicate flower, or a portrait brimming with emotion, you'll have the tools to bring your vision to life on paper.

Moreover, you'll gain practical knowledge about the materials and supplies used in watercolor painting. We'll guide you through selecting quality paints, brushes, and paper, helping you build a versatile toolkit that suits your needs and budget. Understanding your materials is crucial in watercolor, as the interactions between paint, water, and paper can significantly impact your results. With this knowledge, you'll be able to make informed choices and get the most out of your supplies.

One of the most valuable aspects of this book is its emphasis on problem-solving and troubleshooting. Watercolor can be unpredictable, and even experienced artists encounter challenges. We'll teach you how to approach common issues – such as muddy colors, unwanted backruns, or loss of luminosity – with confidence and creativity. You'll learn how to turn mistakes into opportunities for unique effects and how to recover from setbacks without losing the freshness of your painting.

As you work through the exercises and projects in the book, you'll also develop a deeper appreciation for the rich tradition of watercolor painting. We'll introduce you to the works of both historical masters and contemporary artists, providing inspiration and context for your own artistic journey. Understanding the evolution of watercolor as an art form will help you situate your work within a broader artistic context and may inspire you to push the boundaries of the medium in your own unique way.

Perhaps most importantly, this book will help you cultivate patience and mindfulness in your artistic practice. Watercolor, with its fluid nature and need for careful planning, encourages a meditative approach to painting. You'll learn to slow down, observe closely, and make deliberate choices in your work. This mindful approach not only leads to better paintings but can also bring a sense of calm and focus to your daily life.

As you embark on this journey into the world of watercolor, prepare to be challenged, inspired, and delighted. The pages that follow will open up a world of creative possibilities, guiding you step by step through the techniques, principles, and artistic considerations that make watercolor such a beloved medium. Whether you dream of capturing the golden light of a sunset, the delicate petals of a flower, or the emotion in a loved one's face, watercolor offers a beautiful and expressive means of bringing those visions to life.

So, gather your brushes, paints, and paper, and get ready to dive into the enchanting world of watercolor. With "The Art of Watercolor

Made Easy" as your guide, you'll discover the joy of creating luminous, expressive paintings that reflect your unique artistic voice. The journey ahead is filled with colorful adventures, surprising discoveries, and the satisfaction of watching your skills grow with each brushstroke. Let's begin this exciting exploration of transparency, color, and creative expression – your watercolor masterpieces await!

# Chapter 1: Introduction to Watercolor Painting

The history and evolution of watercolor as a medium is a fascinating journey that spans centuries and cultures. Watercolor painting, in its most basic form, can be traced back to prehistoric times when early humans used pigments mixed with water to create cave paintings. However, the refined art of watercolor as we know it today began to take shape during the Renaissance period in Europe.

During the 15th century, artists like Albrecht Dürer started experimenting with watercolor techniques, using them primarily for nature studies and preparatory sketches. These early watercolor works were often seen as supplementary to other mediums, rather than standalone pieces. It wasn't until the 18th century that watercolor began to gain recognition as a serious artistic medium in its own right.

The British school of watercolor painting, which emerged in the late 18th and early 19th centuries, played a crucial role in elevating the status of watercolor. Artists like J.M.W. Turner and John Constable pushed the boundaries of what was possible with watercolor, creating luminous landscapes that captured the imagination of the public and fellow artists alike. Turner, in particular, is often credited with revolutionizing the medium through his innovative techniques and bold use of color.

As renowned art historian Kenneth Clark once noted, "Turner's watercolors are among the greatest works of art ever produced in England, indeed in Europe." This sentiment reflects the growing appreciation for watercolor as a medium capable of producing masterpieces, rather than merely serving as a preparatory tool.

The 19th century saw a further expansion of watercolor's popularity and application. The invention of portable watercolor sets made it easier for artists to paint outdoors, contributing to the rise of plein air painting.

This development allowed artists to capture the fleeting effects of light and atmosphere with unprecedented immediacy and freshness.

In the United States, watercolor gained prominence through the works of artists like Winslow Homer and John Singer Sargent. Homer's seascapes and Sargent's portraits demonstrated the versatility of watercolor, showing that it could be used for a wide range of subjects and styles. The American Watercolor Society, founded in 1866, further promoted the medium and provided a platform for watercolor artists to exhibit their work.

The 20th century brought new innovations and approaches to watercolor painting. Artists like Paul Klee and Wassily Kandinsky incorporated watercolor into their abstract compositions, demonstrating that the medium could be used for more than just representational art. The rise of modernism and abstract expressionism saw watercolor being used in increasingly experimental ways, pushing the boundaries of what was possible with pigment and water.

Today, watercolor continues to evolve and adapt, with contemporary artists exploring new techniques, materials, and subject matter. The medium has also found applications beyond traditional fine art, being used in illustration, design, and even digital art.

The unique characteristics and advantages of watercolor set it apart from other painting mediums. One of its most distinctive features is its transparency, which allows light to reflect off the white paper beneath the paint, creating a luminous quality that is difficult to achieve with other mediums. This transparency also enables artists to build up layers of color, creating depth and complexity in their paintings.

Watercolor's fluidity is another key characteristic that both challenges and delights artists. The way water and pigment interact on paper can create unexpected and often beautiful effects, from soft, blended washes to crisp, defined edges. This unpredictability can be both exciting and daunting for artists, requiring a balance of control and spontaneity.

The portability of watercolor materials is a significant advantage, particularly for artists who enjoy painting outdoors or while traveling. A basic watercolor kit can be compact and lightweight, allowing artists to capture scenes and impressions on the go. This portability has made watercolor a favorite medium for urban sketchers and travel journalers.

Watercolor also offers a unique immediacy. Unlike oil paintings, which can take days or weeks to dry, watercolor paintings dry relatively quickly, allowing artists to work in multiple sessions without long waiting periods. This quick-drying property also makes it easier to layer colors and create glazes, techniques that are fundamental to many watercolor approaches.

The versatility of watercolor is another of its strengths. It can be used for a wide range of styles and subjects, from delicate botanical illustrations to bold abstract compositions. Watercolor can be applied in thin, translucent washes or thick, opaque layers, depending on the artist's intention and technique.

Environmentally conscious artists often appreciate watercolor for its relatively low environmental impact compared to other painting mediums. Water-based paints are generally less toxic than oil-based alternatives, and cleanup requires only water, without the need for harsh solvents.

When it comes to the basic supplies and materials needed for watercolor painting, the list is relatively simple, making it an accessible medium for beginners. The core materials include watercolor paints, brushes, paper, and a few additional tools.

Watercolor paints come in various forms, including pans, tubes, and liquid watercolors. Pan watercolors are solid cakes of pigment that are activated with water, while tube watercolors are in a moist, paste-like form. Liquid watercolors are highly concentrated and come in bottles. For beginners, a basic set of pan or tube watercolors covering the primary colors (red, blue, and yellow) along with a few earth tones is usually sufficient to start exploring the medium.

Brushes are a crucial tool for watercolor painting. While there are many types of brushes available, a few key shapes are essential. Round brushes are versatile and can create both fine lines and broad strokes. Flat brushes are useful for creating washes and straight edges. Many watercolorists also use a large, soft brush called a mop or wash brush for laying down broad areas of color. Natural hair brushes, particularly those made from sable, are traditionally favored for their ability to hold water and create smooth strokes, but high-quality synthetic brushes can also perform well.

The choice of paper is crucial in watercolor painting, as it significantly affects the behavior of the paint and the final appearance of the artwork. Watercolor paper comes in different weights, textures, and compositions. The weight of the paper is measured in grams per square meter (gsm) or pounds per ream, with heavier papers being more durable and less prone to buckling when wet. Common weights include 300 gsm (140 lb) and 640 gsm (300 lb).

Textures in watercolor paper range from smooth (hot-pressed) to rough, with cold-pressed paper offering a middle ground. Each texture interacts differently with the paint, influencing the final look of the artwork. As artist and author Shirley Trevena advises, "Experiment with different papers to find the one that suits your style and technique. The right paper can make a significant difference in your painting experience and results."

Additional tools that can be helpful for watercolor painting include a palette for mixing colors, water containers, a spray bottle for rewetting paints, masking tape for securing paper, and a pencil and eraser for initial sketches. Some artists also use masking fluid to preserve areas of white paper, and sponges or salt for creating textural effects.

When selecting materials, it's important to remember that quality matters, especially when it comes to paints and paper. Artist-grade materials, while more expensive, often produce better results and can be more enjoyable to work with. However, student-grade materials can be a good starting point for beginners who are still exploring the medium.

As you embark on your watercolor journey, remember that the most important tools are patience and practice. Watercolor can be challenging to master, but it's also incredibly rewarding. Each painting is an opportunity to learn and grow as an artist.

The transparency, fluidity, and luminosity of watercolor make it a uniquely expressive medium. As you delve deeper into the world of watercolor, you'll discover its ability to capture light, atmosphere, and emotion in ways that other mediums simply can't match. Whether you're drawn to the delicate washes of botanical illustrations or the bold strokes of abstract landscapes, watercolor offers endless possibilities for artistic expression.

As we move forward in this book, we'll explore the intricacies of watercolor paints, delving into the various types available and the fundamental principles of color theory that will guide your artistic decisions. Understanding these elements will provide you with a solid foundation for your watercolor practice, allowing you to make informed choices about your materials and techniques.

# Chapter 2: Understanding Watercolor Paints

As we delve deeper into the world of watercolor painting, it's crucial to develop a thorough understanding of the paints themselves. The quality, properties, and behavior of your watercolor paints will significantly influence your artistic process and the final appearance of your work. In this chapter, we'll explore the different types of watercolor paints available, delve into color theory and pigment properties, and guide you through creating a basic color palette.

Watercolor paints come in three primary forms: pans, tubes, and liquid. Each of these forms has its own unique characteristics and advantages, catering to different painting styles and preferences.

Pan watercolors are perhaps the most familiar form to many beginners. These are solid cakes of pigment that are activated with water. They come in small, rectangular or circular containers, often arranged in a portable palette. Pan watercolors are prized for their convenience and portability, making them an excellent choice for plein air painting or travel sketching. They're also long-lasting, as the dried paint can be reactivated with water multiple times.

One of the main advantages of pan watercolors is their ease of use. You can control the intensity of the color by adjusting the amount of water you use to activate the paint. This makes it easier to create light washes or build up color gradually. However, pan watercolors can sometimes be less vibrant than their tube or liquid counterparts, particularly if they're student-grade.

Tube watercolors, on the other hand, come in a moist, paste-like form. They're similar to oil paints in their consistency but are water-soluble. Tube watercolors are known for their vibrancy and intensity. They allow for rich, saturated colors and are particularly useful when you need to cover large areas or create bold, dramatic effects.

One of the benefits of tube watercolors is the ability to squeeze out exactly the amount of paint you need, reducing waste. They're also ideal for mixing large quantities of a particular color, which can be useful for consistent washes in larger paintings. However, tube watercolors can dry out if left exposed to air, so it's important to close the tubes tightly after use.

Liquid watercolors are highly concentrated watercolor paints that come in bottles. They're extremely vibrant and flow easily, making them popular for techniques that require a lot of paint and water, such as pouring or creating large washes. Liquid watercolors are also favored by some illustrators and designers for their intensity and ease of application.

The main advantage of liquid watercolors is their ready-to-use nature. There's no need to activate them with water, making them convenient for quick color application. However, they can be more challenging to control than pan or tube watercolors, especially for detailed work.

Renowned watercolor artist Joseph Zbukvic offers this insight: "Each form of watercolor paint has its place in an artist's toolkit. I often use a combination of pan and tube watercolors in my work. The pans are great for quick sketches and adding details, while the tubes allow me to create rich, saturated washes for larger areas."

Regardless of the form you choose, it's essential to understand the properties of the pigments used in watercolor paints. Pigments are the colorants in paint, and their characteristics can significantly affect how the paint behaves on paper.

Pigments can be categorized as either transparent, semi-transparent, or opaque. Transparent pigments allow light to pass through them and reflect off the white paper beneath, creating a luminous effect. These are ideal for glazing techniques and creating depth in your paintings. Semi-transparent pigments partially obscure the layer beneath them, while opaque pigments cover the underlying layers completely.

The transparency of a pigment can greatly influence your painting technique. For instance, transparent colors are excellent for layering and creating subtle color transitions, while opaque colors are useful for creating solid areas of color or for making corrections.

Another important property of pigments is their staining ability. Some pigments, particularly synthetic organic ones, have a tendency to stain the paper, making them difficult to lift or erase once they've dried. Non-staining pigments, on the other hand, can be more easily lifted or adjusted even after they've dried.

Understanding these properties can help you make informed decisions about which paints to use for different effects. For example, you might choose a transparent, non-staining yellow for glazing over other colors, while opting for an opaque, staining blue for creating solid areas of sky.

Color theory is another crucial aspect of understanding watercolor paints. At its most basic, color theory deals with how colors interact with each other and how they can be mixed to create new colors. The color wheel is a fundamental tool in color theory, illustrating the relationships between primary, secondary, and tertiary colors.

The primary colors in traditional color theory are red, blue, and yellow. These are the colors from which all other colors can be mixed. Secondary colors (green, orange, and purple) are created by mixing two primary colors. Tertiary colors are created by mixing a primary color with an adjacent secondary color on the color wheel.

Understanding color relationships can help you create harmonious color schemes in your paintings. Complementary colors, which are opposite each other on the color wheel (such as blue and orange), create vibrant contrasts when used together. Analogous colors, which are next to each other on the color wheel (such as blue, blue-green, and green), create harmonious and soothing color schemes.

Color mixing in watercolor can be more challenging than in other mediums due to the transparent nature of the paints. When mixing watercolors, it's important to remember that the resulting color will often be lighter when it dries. It's also crucial to mix colors with a light touch to avoid creating muddy mixtures.

Artist and author Jean Haines emphasizes the importance of understanding color mixing: "Learning to mix colors effectively is one of the most valuable skills a watercolor artist can develop. It not only expands your palette but also gives you greater control over the mood and atmosphere of your paintings."

Creating a basic color palette is an essential step for any watercolor artist. While it might be tempting to buy every color available, a well-chosen basic palette can provide you with all the colors you need to create a wide range of hues.

A typical basic palette might include the primary colors (a warm and cool version of each), a few earth tones, and one or two convenience colors. Here's an example of what this might look like:
- Warm and cool yellow (e.g., Cadmium Yellow and Lemon Yellow)
- Warm and cool red (e.g., Cadmium Red and Alizarin Crimson)
- Warm and cool blue (e.g., Ultramarine Blue and Phthalo Blue)
- Earth tones (e.g., Yellow Ochre, Burnt Sienna, and Burnt Umber)
- Convenience colors (e.g., Sap Green and Payne's Gray)

This palette allows you to mix a wide range of colors while also providing some ready-made options for common hues. As you become more experienced, you may want to expand your palette to include more specialized colors, but this basic set-up is an excellent starting point.

When selecting paints for your palette, consider factors such as lightfastness (resistance to fading), transparency, and staining properties. Artist-grade paints, while more expensive, often have better lightfastness and more predictable mixing properties than student-grade paints.

Remember, the goal of creating a palette is not to have every color imaginable, but to have a set of colors that work well together and allow you to mix the hues you need. As you develop your style and preferences, your palette will likely evolve to reflect your unique approach to watercolor painting.

Understanding watercolor paints - their types, properties, and how they interact - is fundamental to mastering the medium. This knowledge will inform every aspect of your painting process, from selecting materials to applying paint to paper. As we move forward, we'll explore how to put this knowledge into practice through various watercolor techniques, beginning with the essential methods that form the foundation of watercolor painting.

# Chapter 3: Essential Watercolor Techniques

Having explored the properties of watercolor paints and the principles of color theory, we now turn our attention to the fundamental techniques that form the backbone of watercolor painting. Mastering these essential techniques will provide you with the tools to express your artistic vision and create captivating watercolor paintings.

The wet-on-wet technique is one of the most characteristic and beloved methods in watercolor painting. This technique involves applying wet paint to wet paper or to an area of the paper that has already been wetted with clear water. The result is a soft, diffused effect where colors blend and flow into each other, creating beautiful, organic shapes and gradients.

To execute the wet-on-wet technique, start by wetting your paper with clean water using a large, soft brush or a spray bottle. The paper should be evenly damp but not pooling with water. Then, load your brush with paint and touch it to the wet paper. Watch as the color spreads and blooms across the damp surface. You can add multiple colors, allowing them to mingle and create new hues where they meet.

The wet-on-wet technique is particularly effective for painting skies, water, and other subjects that require soft edges and smooth transitions. It's also excellent for creating atmospheric effects and suggesting distance in landscapes. However, it requires quick work and a certain degree of spontaneity, as the paper will start to dry relatively quickly.

Renowned watercolorist Joseph Zbukvic describes the wet-on-wet technique as "painting with light." He explains, "When you apply paint to wet paper, you're not just adding color, you're manipulating the way light interacts with the paper and pigment. It's a dance between the artist, the paint, and the water."

In contrast to wet-on-wet, the wet-on-dry technique involves applying wet paint to dry paper. This method allows for more control and is ideal for creating defined shapes and hard edges. When you apply wet paint to dry paper, the paint will stay where you put it, allowing you to create precise lines and shapes.

The wet-on-dry technique is versatile and can be used for a wide range of effects. It's particularly useful for adding details, creating texture, and defining specific elements in your painting. For example, you might use wet-on-dry to paint the branches of a tree after creating a soft, wet-on-wet background for the sky.

One of the advantages of the wet-on-dry technique is that it allows you to build up layers of color gradually. You can apply a light wash, let it dry, and then add more intense color on top without the layers blending together. This layering process, known as glazing, is a fundamental aspect of watercolor painting.

Washes are an essential technique in watercolor painting, used to create smooth areas of color. There are three main types of washes: flat washes, graded washes, and variegated washes.

A flat wash is a uniform layer of color applied evenly across an area of the paper. To create a flat wash, mix enough paint to cover the entire area in one go. Tilt your paper at a slight angle and apply the paint from top to bottom in overlapping horizontal strokes. Work quickly to maintain a wet edge, which prevents streaks or hard lines from forming.

Graded washes involve a gradual transition from dark to light (or vice versa) within a single color. To create a graded wash, start with a more concentrated mixture of paint at one end of your paper and gradually dilute it with water as you move towards the other end. This technique is particularly useful for painting skies or suggesting distance in landscapes.

Variegated washes involve using multiple colors that blend together on the paper. To create a variegated wash, apply different colors side by side while the paper is wet, allowing them to mingle and create soft transitions. This technique can create beautiful, atmospheric effects and is often used for painting skies or water.

Glazing is a technique where transparent layers of color are applied over dry underlying layers. Each layer modifies the color beneath it, allowing you to build up rich, complex colors and create depth in your paintings. Glazing requires patience, as each layer must be completely dry before the next is applied.

To glaze effectively, use transparent colors and apply them in thin, even layers. The underlying colors will show through, creating new hues where the glazes overlap. This technique is particularly useful for creating subtle color variations, deepening shadows, or adjusting the overall tone of a painting.

Artist Ann Blockley emphasizes the importance of glazing in her work: "Glazing allows me to build up depth and richness in my paintings gradually. It's like adding layers of atmosphere, each one subtly altering the mood of the piece."

Layering is closely related to glazing but can also involve opaque colors. By building up multiple layers of paint, you can create complex textures and depth in your paintings. Layering can be done wet-on-dry for more control, or wet-on-wet for more organic blending effects.

When layering, it's important to consider the opacity and staining properties of your paints. Some colors will completely cover the layers beneath, while others will allow the underlying colors to show through. Experiment with different combinations to achieve the effects you want.

Creating textures and effects is another essential aspect of watercolor technique. Watercolor lends itself to a wide range of textural effects, many of which take advantage of the medium's fluid nature.

One popular technique for creating texture is salt texturing. By sprinkling salt onto wet paint, you can create interesting patterns as the salt absorbs the water and pushes the pigment away. Once the paint is completely dry, you can brush off the salt to reveal the textured effect beneath.

Splattering is another technique that can add energy and texture to your paintings. Load a brush with paint and tap it against your finger or another brush to create a spray of small dots. This technique can be used to suggest texture in foliage, create a starry sky, or add visual interest to any area of your painting.

Lifting is a technique where you remove paint from the paper to create highlights or correct mistakes. While the paint is still wet, you can lift color by blotting it with a tissue or paper towel. For dry paint, you can rewet the area and lift the color with a damp brush or sponge. Some colors lift more easily than others, so it's important to experiment with your paints to understand their lifting properties.

Renowned watercolorist Alvaro Castagnet emphasizes the importance of these techniques in creating dynamic paintings: "Mastering these essential techniques gives you the tools to capture the essence of your subject. But remember, technique is just the beginning. It's how you apply these techniques creatively that will set your work apart."

As you practice these essential watercolor techniques, you'll begin to develop your own style and preferences. Some artists prefer the loose, fluid effects of wet-on-wet painting, while others gravitate towards the control offered by wet-on-dry techniques. Many successful watercolorists combine multiple techniques within a single painting to achieve their desired effects.

Remember that mastering these techniques takes time and practice. Don't be discouraged if your early attempts don't turn out as you envision - every painting is an opportunity to learn and improve. Keep a sketchbook where you can experiment with different techniques and combinations of colors. This practice will not only help you improve your skills but also aid in developing your unique artistic voice.

As you become more comfortable with these fundamental techniques, you'll be better equipped to tackle more complex subjects and compositions. In the next chapter, we'll explore how to harness these techniques to master one of the most cherished qualities of watercolor: transparency.

25

# Chapter 4: Mastering Transparency

Transparency is often considered the hallmark of watercolor painting, setting it apart from other painting mediums. The ability to create luminous, translucent layers of color that allow the white of the paper to shine through is what gives watercolor its characteristic glow and ethereal quality. Mastering transparency is key to unlocking the full potential of watercolor as a medium.

Controlling the water-to-paint ratio is fundamental to achieving desired levels of transparency in your watercolor paintings. This ratio determines the intensity and opacity of your paint application. A higher proportion of water to paint results in a more transparent wash, while a higher proportion of paint to water creates a more opaque effect.

To create a very transparent wash, start with a small amount of paint on your brush and add plenty of water. This diluted mixture will allow much of the paper's white to show through, creating a soft, luminous effect. As you reduce the amount of water, the color becomes more intense and less transparent.

It's important to note that different pigments have varying levels of natural transparency. Some colors, like Phthalo Blue or Quinacridone Rose, are inherently more transparent, while others, like Cadmium Red or Titanium White, are more opaque. Understanding the properties of your paints will help you predict and control their behavior on paper.

Artist and author Jean Haines emphasizes the importance of this control: "The dance between water and pigment is at the heart of watercolor painting. Learning to control this relationship gives you the power to create everything from the softest, most transparent washes to rich, intense areas of color."

Building up layers for luminous effects is another crucial aspect of mastering transparency in watercolor. This technique, often referred to as glazing, involves applying multiple thin, transparent layers of paint, allowing each layer to dry completely before applying the next.

To begin, apply a very light, transparent wash of color to your paper. Once this is completely dry, apply another transparent layer over the first. Repeat this process, gradually building up the intensity of color. The beauty of this technique is that each layer interacts with the ones beneath it, creating rich, complex colors that seem to glow from within the painting.

When glazing, it's important to work from light to dark and to use transparent colors. Opaque colors can quickly become muddy when layered and may obscure the luminosity you're trying to achieve. Also, be patient and allow each layer to dry completely before adding the next. If you apply a new layer to a partially dry wash, you risk lifting or disturbing the underlying layers.

Renowned watercolorist Alvaro Castagnet describes the glazing process as "building atmosphere" in a painting. He says, "Each transparent layer adds depth and richness to the painting. It's like adding veils of color, each one subtly altering the mood and atmosphere of the piece."

Preserving white space and highlights is another crucial skill in mastering transparency in watercolor. The white of the paper serves as the brightest highlight in a watercolor painting, and learning to preserve and utilize this white space is essential for creating luminous effects.

One technique for preserving whites is simply to paint around the areas you want to keep white. This requires careful planning and a steady hand. Another method is to use masking fluid, a liquid rubber solution that can be applied to areas you want to keep white. Once the masking fluid is dry, you can paint freely over it. When you're finished painting and the paint is dry, you can rub off the masking fluid to reveal pristine white paper beneath.

For smaller highlights, you can also lift paint while it's still wet using a clean, damp brush or a paper towel. This technique allows you to create soft-edged highlights or to correct areas where you may have accidentally painted over a spot you intended to keep white.

Artist and instructor Brenda Swenson emphasizes the importance of white space in watercolor: "The white of the paper is your brightest white. No paint can match its luminosity. Learning to preserve and utilize this white space is crucial for creating paintings that glow with light."

Understanding the concept of negative painting is also crucial when working with transparency in watercolor. Negative painting involves defining a shape by painting around it rather than painting the shape itself. This technique is particularly useful for creating the illusion of light and preserving the luminosity of your painting.

For example, if you're painting a tree in front of a bright sky, you might start by painting a light wash for the sky, leaving the shape of the tree unpainted. Then, you would paint around the tree shape with progressively darker washes, defining its form by painting the negative space around it. This approach allows you to maintain the luminosity of the paper for the brightest areas of your painting.

Negative painting can be challenging at first, as it requires you to think about shapes and spaces in a different way. However, mastering this technique can greatly enhance your ability to create luminous, transparent effects in your watercolor paintings.

Another important aspect of mastering transparency is understanding how different papers affect the luminosity of your painting. The texture and absorbency of the paper can significantly impact how light interacts with your paint layers.

Hot-pressed paper, which has a smooth surface, tends to allow paint to sit on top of the paper more, potentially creating more luminous effects. Cold-pressed paper, with its slightly textured surface, can create interesting interactions between the paint and the paper's texture, adding depth to your transparent washes. Rough paper, with its pronounced texture, can create beautiful granulation effects with certain pigments, adding another dimension to your transparent layers.

Experimenting with different paper types can help you find the surface that best supports your painting style and the luminous effects you want to achieve.

As you work on mastering transparency in your watercolor paintings, remember that it's not just about technical skill, but also about developing an eye for where and how to use transparent effects to enhance your work. Sometimes, a painting may benefit from areas of more opaque paint to provide contrast and visual interest.

Watercolor artist Thomas W. Schaller advises, "Transparency in watercolor is not just about technique, it's about seeing. It's about understanding how light interacts with your subject and using the unique properties of watercolor to capture that interaction on paper."

Practice is key to mastering transparency in watercolor. Experiment with different water-to-paint ratios, try glazing with various color combinations, and explore different ways of preserving white space in your paintings. Keep a journal of your experiments, noting which techniques and color combinations produce the effects you like best.

Remember that mastering transparency is an ongoing process. Even experienced watercolorists continue to discover new ways to use transparency in their work. Embrace the learning process and don't be afraid to make mistakes – often, these "mistakes" can lead to unexpected and beautiful effects.

As you continue to develop your skills in creating transparent effects, you'll find that your watercolor paintings take on a new level of depth and luminosity. This mastery of transparency will serve you well as we move on to explore composition and design in watercolor painting, where the interplay of transparent and opaque areas can greatly enhance the overall impact of your work.

# Chapter 5: Composition and Design in Watercolor

As we transition from mastering the fundamental techniques of watercolor painting, we now turn our attention to the crucial elements of composition and design. These principles form the backbone of any successful painting, guiding the viewer's eye and creating a harmonious visual experience. In this chapter, we will explore the basic principles of composition, delve into the effective use of value and contrast, and learn how to plan and sketch your painting for optimal results.

## Basic principles of composition

The art of composition is as old as art itself, with roots tracing back to ancient civilizations. In watercolor painting, as in all visual arts, composition serves as the framework upon which we build our artistic vision. It is the arrangement of elements within the picture plane that creates a cohesive and visually appealing image. Understanding and applying these principles can elevate your watercolor paintings from mere representations to captivating works of art.

One of the most fundamental principles of composition is the rule of thirds. This guideline suggests dividing your canvas into a 3x3 grid and placing key elements along these lines or at their intersections. By doing so, you create a more balanced and dynamic composition that naturally draws the viewer's eye. Consider the words of renowned watercolorist Joseph Zbukvic: "The rule of thirds is not a rigid law, but rather a starting point for creating interesting compositions. It's a tool that helps artists avoid centering everything, which often results in static and uninteresting paintings."

Another essential principle is the concept of balance. In watercolor painting, balance doesn't necessarily mean symmetry. Instead, it refers to the visual weight of elements within your composition. This can be achieved through the distribution of dark and light areas, the placement of large and small objects, or the use of warm and cool colors. A well-balanced composition feels stable and harmonious, even when it's asymmetrical.

The principle of contrast is equally important in creating compelling watercolor compositions. Contrast can be achieved through various means, such as differences in size, shape, color, or value. By incorporating contrasting elements, you create visual interest and guide the viewer's eye through the painting. For instance, a small, bright object placed against a large, dark background can become a powerful focal point.

Leading lines are another powerful compositional tool in watercolor painting. These are visual pathways that guide the viewer's eye through the painting, often leading to the focal point. Leading lines can be explicit, such as a winding road or a river, or implicit, created by the arrangement of objects or the direction of brushstrokes. As you plan your composition, consider how you can use leading lines to create a sense of movement and direct attention to key areas of your painting.

The concept of unity is crucial in creating a cohesive watercolor composition. Unity ensures that all elements in your painting work together to create a harmonious whole. This can be achieved through repetition of colors, shapes, or textures, or through a consistent style or theme throughout the painting. As watercolor artist John Salminen notes, "A unified composition feels complete and satisfying. It's as if every element belongs exactly where it is, contributing to the overall impact of the painting."

Negative space, often overlooked by beginners, plays a vital role in watercolor composition. This is the space around and between the main subjects of your painting. Effective use of negative space can enhance the impact of your focal points, create a sense of balance, and add depth to your composition. In watercolor painting, the white of the paper often serves as negative space, making it particularly important to plan and preserve these areas.

The principle of emphasis helps you guide the viewer's attention to the most important elements of your painting. This can be achieved through various means, such as placing the focal point at a strategic location (like one of the intersections in the rule of thirds), using contrasting colors or values, or employing more detail in the area you want to emphasize. Remember, emphasis doesn't mean that everything else in your painting should be dull or uninteresting. Rather, it's about creating a hierarchy of visual interest that leads the viewer through your composition.

As you apply these principles of composition to your watercolor paintings, it's important to remember that they are guidelines, not rigid rules. The true art lies in understanding these principles and then knowing when and how to break them for creative effect. As you gain experience, you'll develop an intuitive sense of composition that allows you to create balanced, harmonious paintings that effectively convey your artistic vision.

## Using value and contrast effectively

Value, the relative lightness or darkness of a color, is a fundamental element in watercolor painting that can make or break your composition. Understanding and effectively using value is crucial for creating depth, form, and atmosphere in your paintings. In watercolor, value is particularly important because the transparency of the medium allows light to reflect off the white paper beneath, creating luminous effects that are unique to this medium.

One of the most effective ways to use value in watercolor is through the creation of a value scale. This is a gradual progression from the lightest value (the white of the paper) to the darkest value your pigments can produce. By understanding and being able to reproduce this scale, you can more effectively plan and execute the values in your painting. As watercolor master Charles Reid advises, "Squint at your subject. This helps you see the basic value patterns without being distracted by details or color."

Contrast, the difference between light and dark values, is a powerful tool for creating impact and guiding the viewer's eye in your watercolor paintings. High contrast areas naturally draw attention, while areas of low contrast tend to recede. By strategically placing areas of high and low contrast, you can create a sense of depth and hierarchy in your composition.

One effective technique for using value and contrast in watercolor is the notan study. Notan is a Japanese word that refers to the balance between light and dark. A notan study simplifies your composition into two or three values, helping you see the overall structure and balance of your painting before you begin. This can be particularly helpful in watercolor, where preserving light areas is crucial and can be challenging to correct later.

Another important consideration when working with value in watercolor is the concept of atmospheric perspective. This refers to the way objects appear lighter and less detailed as they recede into the distance. By gradually decreasing the contrast and lightening the values of distant objects, you can create a convincing sense of depth and atmosphere in your landscapes.

The effective use of value and contrast also plays a crucial role in creating form and volume in your watercolor paintings. By understanding how light falls on objects and creates shadows, you can use value to model three-dimensional forms on your two-dimensional paper. This is particularly important in still life and portrait painting, where capturing the subtleties of light and shadow can bring your subjects to life.

It's important to note that in watercolor, achieving dark values can be challenging. Unlike opaque mediums where you can simply add black paint, in watercolor, you need to build up layers of pigment to create deep, rich darks. This requires patience and practice, but the results can be stunning. As watercolor artist Joseph Zbukvic notes, "The darkest darks in a watercolor painting should still have a translucent quality. This is what gives watercolor its unique luminosity."

When planning your value structure, consider the overall mood you want to convey in your painting. A high-key painting with predominantly light values can create a bright, cheerful atmosphere, while a low-key painting with predominantly dark values can evoke a more somber or mysterious mood. The distribution of values in your composition can dramatically affect the emotional impact of your painting.

Remember that value is independent of color. Two different colors can have the same value, and the same color can have different values depending on how much water you add. This is why many artists find it helpful to work from black and white reference photos or to convert their color references to grayscale when planning their value structure.

As you work on incorporating effective value and contrast into your watercolor paintings, practice seeing your subjects in terms of value rather than color. This skill, often called "value sight," is crucial for creating strong compositions and can significantly improve the impact of your paintings. With time and practice, you'll develop an intuitive understanding of how to use value and contrast to create compelling watercolor compositions that captivate viewers and effectively convey your artistic vision.

## Planning and sketching your painting

The planning and sketching phase is a crucial step in the watercolor painting process, often determining the success of the final piece. This preparatory work allows you to resolve compositional issues, experiment with different arrangements, and plan your color scheme before committing paint to paper. As renowned watercolorist Alvaro Castagnet puts it, "A good painting is 90% planning and 10% execution."

The first step in planning your watercolor painting is to clearly define your concept or vision. What is the main idea or feeling you want to convey? What elements are essential to telling your story? Having a clear vision will guide your decisions throughout the planning and painting process. This might involve making quick thumbnail sketches to explore different compositions or writing down key words that capture the essence of what you want to express.

Once you have a general idea, it's time to create more detailed sketches. These sketches serve multiple purposes: they help you refine your composition, plan your value structure, and serve as a guide when you begin painting. Many watercolor artists prefer to work from life or from their own reference photos, as this allows for a more personal and authentic interpretation of the subject.

When sketching for a watercolor painting, it's important to keep your lines light and loose. Heavy, dark lines can show through your washes and detract from the final painting. Instead, use gentle pencil strokes that can be easily erased or will disappear under your paint layers. Some artists prefer to use a light blue or sepia pencil for their initial sketches, as these colors blend well with most watercolor palettes.

As you sketch, pay attention to the overall shapes and proportions of your subject. Simplify complex forms into basic geometric shapes - this will help you capture the essence of your subject without getting bogged down in details too early. Remember, your sketch is a roadmap for your painting, not a detailed rendering.

During the sketching phase, it's also helpful to plan your value structure. Create a small value sketch alongside your main sketch, simplifying your composition into three to five values. This will help you establish a strong foundation for your painting and ensure a cohesive overall design.

Another important aspect of planning your watercolor painting is deciding on your color scheme. While you don't need to plan every single color you'll use, having a general idea of your palette can help create a harmonious final painting. Consider creating a small color study to experiment with different combinations and see how they interact with each other.

Many watercolor artists find it helpful to create a detailed drawing on a separate piece of paper, which they then transfer to their watercolor paper using transfer paper or by redrawing it lightly. This allows for more experimentation and refinement without damaging the surface of the watercolor paper.

When planning your painting, consider the unique properties of watercolor. Unlike opaque mediums, watercolor requires you to plan for preserving the white of the paper for your lightest values. This might involve using masking fluid or carefully planning your brush strokes to leave certain areas untouched. As you sketch, make note of areas that need to remain white or very light.

It's also important to plan the sequence of your painting. In watercolor, it's generally easier to work from light to dark and from large shapes to small details. Sketch out a rough plan of which areas you'll paint first and how you'll layer your washes. This can help prevent muddy colors and preserve the freshness and spontaneity that makes watercolor so appealing.

Don't forget to plan for happy accidents - one of the joys of watercolor is its unpredictability. Leave room in your planning for spontaneous effects and be prepared to adapt your plan as your painting develops. As watercolor master Joseph Zbukvic advises, "Plan thoroughly, but paint with abandon."

Remember, planning and sketching are not about creating a rigid blueprint for your painting. Rather, they're about exploring possibilities, solving problems before they arise, and giving yourself a strong foundation from which to create. The goal is to free your mind to focus on the act of painting itself, allowing for those magical moments of intuition and spontaneity that make watercolor such a rewarding medium.

As we conclude this chapter on composition and design in watercolor, it's clear that these elements form the backbone of successful paintings. By understanding and applying the basic principles of composition, effectively using value and contrast, and thoroughly planning and sketching your work, you'll be well-equipped to create compelling watercolor paintings that engage viewers and effectively communicate your artistic vision. In the next chapter, we'll explore how to apply these principles specifically to landscape painting, one of the most popular and rewarding subjects in watercolor.

# Chapter 6: Painting Landscapes in Watercolor

As we transition from the foundational principles of composition and design explored in the previous chapter, we now turn our attention to one of the most beloved subjects in watercolor painting: landscapes. The natural world offers an endless array of inspiration, from majestic mountain ranges to serene coastal scenes. In this chapter, we will delve into the techniques and approaches that will enable you to capture the essence of landscapes in your watercolor paintings.

## Capturing Skies and Clouds

The sky often serves as the backdrop for landscape paintings, setting the mood and atmosphere for the entire composition. Mastering the art of painting skies and clouds in watercolor is essential for creating compelling landscape works.

To begin, consider the time of day and weather conditions you wish to depict. A clear, sunny day will require different techniques and color choices compared to a stormy or overcast sky. Start by wetting your paper thoroughly for a wet-on-wet technique, which allows colors to blend seamlessly. For a bright, clear sky, use a mixture of cerulean blue and a touch of cobalt blue, applying it with broad, horizontal strokes. As you move towards the horizon, gradually dilute the mixture with more water to create a sense of atmospheric perspective.

Clouds present a unique challenge in watercolor due to their soft, ethereal nature. To paint cumulus clouds, leave areas of white paper untouched while painting the sky around them. Once the initial wash is dry, use a damp brush to softly blend the edges of the clouds, creating a three-dimensional effect. For wispy cirrus clouds, use a dry brush technique with a very light touch, dragging a nearly dry brush loaded with diluted white or pale blue across the paper.

Renowned watercolor artist Joseph Zbukvic once said, "The sky is the engine room of the landscape. Get that right, and you're halfway there." This sentiment underscores the importance of mastering sky techniques in landscape painting. Practice various sky conditions, from dramatic sunsets to misty mornings, to expand your repertoire and bring depth to your landscapes.

## Depicting Water and Reflections

Water features, whether a tranquil lake, a babbling brook, or a vast ocean, add a dynamic element to landscape paintings. The key to successfully depicting water lies in understanding how it interacts with light and its surroundings.

For still water bodies like lakes or ponds, begin with a pale wash that reflects the color of the sky. Once dry, add horizontal strokes of slightly darker values to suggest ripples or subtle movement. To create reflections, paint inverted images of the surrounding landscape elements directly below their counterparts, using slightly muted colors. Remember that reflections are often softer and less detailed than the objects they mirror.

Moving water, such as rivers or waterfalls, requires a different approach. Use directional brushstrokes that follow the flow of the water. For rapids or waterfalls, leave areas of white paper to represent foam or spray, and use darker values in the shadows to create depth. Experiment with lifting techniques to create highlights and suggest the movement of water over rocks.

One of the most challenging aspects of painting water is capturing its transparency. To achieve this effect, build up layers of transparent washes, allowing each layer to dry completely before applying the next. This technique allows the underlying colors to show through, creating the illusion of depth and clarity.

American watercolorist John Singer Sargent, known for his masterful depictions of water, once remarked, "To paint water, you must understand its essence – its fluidity, its reflective nature, and its constant motion." This insight reminds us to observe water carefully in nature, studying how it behaves under different lighting conditions and in various settings.

## Rendering Trees, Mountains, and Foliage

Trees and foliage are integral elements in most landscape paintings, providing structure, texture, and a sense of scale. When painting trees, consider their overall shape and form before focusing on individual leaves or branches. Begin with a light wash to establish the basic shape and local color of the tree. Once dry, use a smaller brush to add branches and define the structure of the tree.

For deciduous trees with full foliage, use a combination of wet-on-wet and dry brush techniques to create a sense of mass and texture. Start with a wet wash for the main body of leaves, then add darker values and details with a dry brush once the initial layer is dry. For coniferous trees, use upward-pointing brushstrokes to suggest the texture of needles, gradually darkening the values towards the base of the tree to create depth.

Mountains present a unique challenge in landscape painting due to their massive scale and complex textures. Begin by establishing the basic shapes of the mountain range with a light wash. As you move towards the foreground, gradually increase the intensity of colors and level of detail. Use the principle of atmospheric perspective, making distant mountains appear cooler and less detailed than those in the foreground.

To create the illusion of rugged terrain, employ a dry brush technique to suggest rocky outcrops and crevices. Pay attention to the way light falls on the mountainside, using warmer colors for sunlit areas and cooler shadows. Remember that snow-capped peaks require careful preservation of white paper, with subtle blue or gray shadows to define their form.

Foliage in the foreground of your landscape requires more detailed treatment than distant vegetation. Use a variety of brushstrokes and techniques to suggest different types of plants and grasses. For example, tall grasses can be painted with vertical strokes of varying lengths, while bushes might require a more rounded, dabbing technique.

English watercolorist David Curtis offers valuable advice on painting vegetation: "Don't try to paint every leaf. Instead, capture the essence of the foliage through shape, color, and texture." This approach allows for a more expressive and less labored representation of natural elements in your landscape.

As you practice rendering these various landscape elements, you'll develop a deeper understanding of how they interact with light and atmosphere. This knowledge will enable you to create more convincing and evocative landscape paintings.

The art of landscape painting in watercolor is a journey of constant observation and practice. Each landscape presents unique challenges and opportunities for artistic expression. As you continue to explore this genre, you'll find that the techniques learned here can be combined and adapted to capture the infinite variety of natural scenes.

Remember that the goal is not to create a photorealistic reproduction of a landscape, but rather to convey its essence and the emotions it evokes. Allow yourself the freedom to interpret the scene before you, emphasizing certain elements and simplifying others to create a cohesive and compelling composition.

As we conclude our exploration of landscape painting, we look ahead to the next chapter, where we will delve into the delicate world of still life and floral watercolors. The skills you've developed in capturing the grand vistas of landscapes will serve you well as we turn our attention to more intimate subjects, examining how to render the subtle textures and intricate details of flowers and everyday objects.

# Chapter 7: Still Life and Floral Watercolors

As we transition from the expansive landscapes explored in the previous chapter, we now turn our attention to the intimate world of still life and floral subjects. These genres have long been staples of watercolor painting, offering artists the opportunity to capture the delicate beauty of everyday objects and the fleeting splendor of nature's blooms. In this chapter, we will delve into the techniques and approaches that will enable you to create stunning still life and floral compositions, bringing to life the subtle interplay of light, color, and form that defines these subjects.

## Painting Fruits and Vegetables

The humble fruit bowl has been a favorite subject of artists for centuries, and with good reason. Fruits and vegetables offer a diverse array of shapes, colors, and textures that provide endless possibilities for exploration in watercolor. When approaching a still life composition featuring produce, it's essential to begin with careful observation. Take time to study the unique characteristics of each item - the smooth, waxy surface of an apple, the dimpled skin of an orange, or the complex geometry of a pineapple.

To capture the essence of fruits and vegetables in watercolor, start with a light sketch to establish the basic forms and composition. As you begin to apply paint, consider the layering process that will build up the depth and richness of color. For many fruits, it's effective to begin with a base wash of a lighter hue, allowing it to dry before adding subsequent layers. This technique can create the illusion of the fruit's inner flesh showing through its skin.

When painting an apple, for instance, you might start with a pale yellow wash across the entire form. Once dry, apply a red or green glaze, leaving some areas of the yellow underpainting visible to suggest highlights. To add dimension, use darker tones of the same color family in the shadowed areas, gradually building up the intensity. Remember that the key to realistic fruit is not just in the color, but in the subtle variations of tone that suggest its three-dimensional form.

Vegetables often present more complex textures and structures. Consider the layers of an onion or the ridges of a bell pepper. These details can be achieved through a combination of wet-on-wet techniques for soft transitions and wet-on-dry for more defined edges. Don't be afraid to use negative painting techniques to define the contours and create separation between overlapping forms.

As you work on your still life, pay close attention to the play of light across the surfaces of your subjects. Highlights can be created by leaving areas of the paper white or by lifting color with a damp brush. Shadows, on the other hand, should be rendered with transparent washes that allow the underlying colors to show through, maintaining the characteristic luminosity of watercolor.

## Capturing the Delicacy of Flowers

Flowers present a unique challenge and opportunity for watercolor artists. Their delicate petals, intricate structures, and vibrant colors seem tailor-made for the medium, yet capturing their essence requires a deft touch and a nuanced approach. As the renowned botanical artist Margaret Mee once said, "To paint flowers, you have to love them and understand them."

When painting flowers, begin by studying your subject closely. Observe how the petals overlap, how they catch the light, and how their colors shift from the center outwards. Start with a loose, gestural sketch to capture the overall form and energy of the flower. This initial sketch should be light, as it will serve as a guide for your painting rather than a rigid structure.

For many flowers, a wet-on-wet approach can be highly effective in capturing the soft, organic nature of petals. Begin by wetting the area where you'll paint the flower, then drop in color, allowing it to bloom and spread naturally across the damp paper. This technique is particularly useful for creating soft edges and gentle color transitions that are characteristic of many blooms.

As you build up the flower, consider the layering of petals. Start with the petals that are furthest back, gradually working your way forward. This approach will help create a sense of depth and dimension in your painting. Use varying degrees of pigment concentration to suggest the transparency of petals, with more diluted washes for areas where light passes through the flower.

For more structured flowers, such as roses or tulips, you may need to employ a combination of wet-on-wet and wet-on-dry techniques. Use wet-on-wet for the softer areas of petals, and switch to wet-on-dry for defining edges and creating more precise details. Remember that even in more structured flowers, there's rarely a need for hard edges - the beauty of watercolor lies in its ability to suggest rather than explicitly define.

Color plays a crucial role in floral painting. While it's important to observe and represent the actual colors of your subject, don't be afraid to exaggerate or adjust hues to create a more harmonious or expressive composition. Consider using complementary colors to make your flowers pop - for instance, adding touches of purple to the shadows of yellow daffodils, or hints of green in the depths of red roses.

As you work, be mindful of preserving highlights. The way light catches on the curved surface of a petal can bring your flower to life. These highlights can be created by leaving areas of white paper or by lifting color with a clean, damp brush. For very small, bright highlights, a touch of white gouache can be used sparingly as a final accent.

## Creating Depth and Dimension in Still Life Compositions

While individual objects in a still life are important, the true art lies in creating a cohesive composition that draws the viewer in and guides their eye through the painting. Depth and dimension are key elements in achieving this, transforming a collection of objects into a compelling visual narrative.

To create depth in your still life compositions, consider the arrangement of your objects carefully. Place some items in the foreground, others in the middle ground, and perhaps suggest additional elements in the background. This layering of space will immediately give your painting a sense of three-dimensionality.

As you begin to paint, pay close attention to the relative values of your objects. Items in the foreground should generally have the highest contrast and most detail, while those further back may be rendered with softer edges and less distinct features. This gradual reduction in detail and contrast as objects recede into the background is known as atmospheric perspective, and it's a powerful tool for creating the illusion of depth.

The use of shadows is crucial in grounding your objects and creating a sense of space. Cast shadows connect objects to their surroundings and to each other, enhancing the three-dimensional quality of your painting. When rendering shadows, remember that they are not simply dark areas - they reflect the colors of surrounding objects and the ambient light. Use transparent washes of color to suggest these subtle variations.

Consider the background of your still life carefully. While it's tempting to leave it as plain white paper, a thoughtfully rendered background can significantly enhance the depth and mood of your painting. A graduated wash can suggest a wall or tabletop, while more complex backgrounds might include drapery or glimpses of additional objects. Whatever you choose, ensure that it complements rather than competes with your main subjects.

Overlapping is another effective technique for creating depth. Allow some objects to partially obscure others, reinforcing the spatial relationships between them. This can be particularly effective with translucent objects like glass, where you can see hints of the objects behind them.

As you develop your still life, don't be afraid to make adjustments to your composition. The beauty of watercolor is its fluidity, both literally and figuratively. If you find that an object isn't working in its current position, you can often lift much of the paint and move it, or simply paint over it if it's in the background. Remember the words of artist Edgar Degas: "Art is not what you see, but what you make others see."

In creating dimension, consider the form of each object carefully. Use a range of values to suggest the way light wraps around curved surfaces. For spherical objects like apples or rounded vases, the transition from light to shadow should be gradual. For objects with flat planes, like books or boxes, the shift in value may be more abrupt.

Texture can also play a significant role in creating dimension. The smooth surface of a polished apple will reflect light differently than the rough skin of a lemon or the velvety petals of a rose. Use a combination of techniques - dry brush for rough textures, wet-in-wet for soft transitions, and glazing for smooth surfaces - to capture these variations.

Finally, consider the overall composition in terms of balance and focus. Use the principles of design we discussed in earlier chapters to create a harmonious arrangement. Lead the viewer's eye through the painting with thoughtful placement of objects, use of color, and control of edges. Remember that negative space - the areas between and around your objects - is just as important as the objects themselves in creating a balanced composition.

As we conclude our exploration of still life and floral watercolors, take a moment to reflect on the unique challenges and joys of these subjects. They offer endless opportunities for experimentation and growth, allowing you to hone your skills in observation, color mixing, and technique. Whether you're capturing the translucent petals of a delicate orchid or the robust form of a ripe pear, each painting is an opportunity to celebrate the beauty of the everyday world around us.

In the next chapter, we'll turn our attention to perhaps the most challenging and rewarding subject in watercolor painting: the human form. We'll explore techniques for capturing the subtleties of skin tones, the expressiveness of faces, and the complex textures of clothing and fabric. As we move forward, carry with you the lessons learned from still life and floral painting - the importance of careful observation, the power of layering and glazing, and the endless possibilities that watercolor offers for capturing the world in all its vibrant, luminous beauty.

# Chapter 8: Portraits and Figure Painting

As we transition from the delicate intricacies of still life and floral watercolors, we now turn our attention to one of the most challenging yet rewarding subjects in watercolor painting: the human form. Portraits and figure painting have long been considered the pinnacle of artistic achievement, and watercolor offers a unique medium to capture the essence of humanity with its characteristic luminosity and fluidity.

Mixing skin tones in watercolor is an art in itself, requiring a nuanced understanding of color theory and pigment properties. Unlike other mediums, watercolor demands a light touch and careful layering to achieve the subtle variations in human skin. The key lies in understanding that skin is not a single flat color, but a complex interplay of warm and cool tones, affected by light, shadow, and the underlying structure of bone and muscle.

To begin, it's essential to recognize that there is no one-size-fits-all approach to skin tones. Every individual's skin is unique, influenced by genetics, environment, and even emotional states. As John Singer Sargent, the master watercolorist, once said, "A portrait is a painting with something wrong with the mouth." This humorous observation underscores the complexity of capturing not just the physical likeness, but the character and essence of a subject.

When mixing skin tones, start with a basic palette of warm and cool colors. A typical combination might include yellow ochre, cadmium red light, and ultramarine blue. The proportions of these colors will vary depending on the specific skin tone you're aiming to achieve. For lighter skin tones, you might lean more heavily on yellow ochre with touches of cadmium red. For darker skin tones, increase the proportion of ultramarine blue and cadmium red.

It's crucial to remember that less is more when it comes to watercolor. Start with very diluted washes, gradually building up the color. This approach allows for greater control and prevents the muddy effect that can occur when too much pigment is applied at once. As you layer, pay attention to the areas where the skin appears cooler or warmer. For instance, areas around the eyes, under the chin, and in the shadows of facial contours often have cooler undertones, while cheeks, nose, and forehead tend to be warmer.

One technique that can be particularly effective in achieving realistic skin tones is glazing. This involves applying thin, transparent layers of color over a dry underpainting. By using complementary colors in your glazes, you can create depth and vibrancy in the skin. For example, a light glaze of purple over a warm skin tone can add a lifelike quality to the shadows.

As you work on mixing skin tones, it's important to constantly observe and compare. Look at the subject (or reference photo) with a critical eye, noting the subtle shifts in color across the face or body. Don't be afraid to experiment with unexpected colors. A touch of green in the shadow areas or a hint of blue in the highlights can add surprising depth to your portrait.

Moving on to capturing facial features and expressions, we enter the realm where technical skill meets artistic interpretation. The eyes, often called the windows to the soul, are perhaps the most crucial element in a portrait. They not only need to be anatomically correct but must also convey the subject's personality and emotional state.

When painting eyes, begin with the overall shape, including the eye socket. Use light washes to establish the basic form, then gradually add detail. The iris is particularly challenging in watercolor, as it requires both precision and a delicate touch. Start with a light wash for the base color of the iris, then use a finer brush to add the intricate patterns and darker tones around the pupil. Remember to leave a small white highlight to give the eye a lifelike sparkle.

The nose and mouth present their own challenges. The nose is primarily about form and shadow rather than detailed features. Use subtle changes in tone to suggest its three-dimensional shape. The mouth, on the other hand, is all about subtle color variations and the play of light on the lips. Observe how the upper lip is often in shadow, while the lower lip catches the light.

Expressions are where your portrait truly comes to life. It's not just about the arrangement of features, but how they interact to convey emotion. A slight lift of an eyebrow, a hint of a smile, or a furrowed brow can completely change the mood of a portrait. Study the works of great watercolor portraitists like Charles Reid, who said, "I'm not interested in making a photographic image. I want to make a statement about the person."

When working on expressions, resist the urge to overwork the painting. Sometimes, a few well-placed brushstrokes can convey more emotion than a highly detailed rendering. This is where the unique qualities of watercolor shine. The medium's fluidity allows for spontaneous marks that can capture the fleeting nature of expression in a way that other media cannot.

As we move from the face to the rest of the figure, depicting clothing and fabric textures becomes our next challenge. Clothing not only adds visual interest to a portrait or figure painting but also provides important context and can be a powerful tool for characterization.

The key to successfully rendering fabric in watercolor lies in understanding how different materials interact with light. Silk, for instance, has a sheen that creates sharp highlights and deep shadows. Cotton, on the other hand, has a softer, more matte appearance. Before you begin painting, take time to observe how light falls on different fabrics. Notice the folds, creases, and how the material drapes over the body.

When painting clothing, start with broad washes to establish the base color and overall form. Pay attention to the large shapes created by areas of light and shadow. Once this foundation is dry, begin to add details such as folds and textures. For crisp fabrics like starched shirts or structured jackets, use more defined brushstrokes and harder edges. For softer materials like wool or velvet, employ a softer touch with blended edges.

One technique that can be particularly effective for rendering fabric textures is dry brush. This involves using a brush with very little water and dragging it across the surface of the paper. The resulting broken texture can be perfect for suggesting the weave of rough fabrics or the fuzzy surface of wool.

Color plays a crucial role in depicting fabric convincingly. Observe how the local color of the fabric is affected by light and shadow. Even a white shirt will have areas of cool and warm tones depending on the lighting conditions. Don't be afraid to use unexpected colors in your shadows or highlights to bring the fabric to life.

Folds and creases in fabric can be one of the most challenging aspects to capture in watercolor. The key is to think in terms of planes rather than lines. Each fold creates a new surface that catches light differently. Use value changes to suggest these planes, reserving your darkest values for the deepest creases.

As you work on clothing, remember that it should enhance, not overpower, your portrait or figure. The fabric should feel like a natural extension of the person, not a separate entity. Pay attention to how the clothing interacts with the body beneath it. A well-executed piece of clothing can reveal much about the form and posture of your subject.

Throughout the process of painting portraits and figures in watercolor, it's important to maintain a balance between accuracy and artistic expression. While anatomical correctness is important, don't let it stifle your creativity. As the renowned watercolorist Joseph Zbukvic aptly put it, "Technique is important, but it's only a tool. The real art is in seeing and feeling."

Remember that every brushstroke is an opportunity to convey something about your subject. The way you handle the paint, the colors you choose, and the details you emphasize all contribute to the story you're telling about the person in your painting.

As we conclude this chapter on portraits and figure painting, it's worth reflecting on the unique challenges and rewards this subject matter offers. Watercolor, with its transparency and unpredictability, may seem at odds with the precision often associated with portraiture. However, it's precisely these qualities that allow for a fresh, vibrant approach to capturing the human form.

The skills you've developed in mixing skin tones, capturing facial features and expressions, and depicting clothing and fabric textures will serve you well beyond portraiture. These techniques can be applied to any subject matter that involves the human figure, from bustling street scenes to intimate domestic moments.

As we move forward to the next chapter on advanced watercolor techniques, keep in mind that the human form offers endless opportunities for exploration and expression. The techniques we'll discuss, such as negative painting and lifting, can be particularly effective when applied to portraits and figures, adding another layer of sophistication to your work.

# Chapter 9: Advanced Watercolor Techniques

As we delve deeper into the world of watercolor painting, it's time to explore some of the more advanced techniques that can elevate your artwork to new heights. These methods will not only expand your creative toolkit but also challenge you to think differently about how you approach your paintings. In this chapter, we'll explore negative painting, lifting techniques, the use of masking fluid, and the incorporation of mixed media elements. These advanced techniques will help you push the boundaries of traditional watercolor painting and develop a more sophisticated and nuanced approach to your art.

## Negative Painting and Lifting Techniques

Negative painting is a technique that involves painting around a subject rather than directly painting the subject itself. This method allows you to create interesting shapes and forms by defining the space around them, rather than the objects themselves. It's a powerful tool for creating depth and dimension in your paintings, and it can be particularly effective when working with complex subjects or intricate patterns.

To begin exploring negative painting, start by identifying the shapes you want to preserve in your composition. These could be the silhouettes of trees against a sunset sky, the outlines of flowers in a garden, or the forms of buildings in a cityscape. Once you've identified these shapes, you'll paint around them, gradually building up layers of color and tone to define the negative space.

One of the key challenges of negative painting is maintaining the edges of your preserved shapes as you work. This requires careful control of your brush and paint application. Start with lighter washes and gradually build up to darker, more saturated colors. As you work, pay close attention to the edges of your negative shapes, using a clean, damp brush to soften any hard lines or to lift color if needed.

Speaking of lifting color, this is another advanced technique that can add depth and nuance to your watercolor paintings. Lifting involves removing pigment from the paper after it has been applied, either while it's still wet or after it has dried. This technique can be used to create highlights, adjust values, or add texture to your painting.

There are several methods for lifting color. One common approach is to use a clean, damp brush to gently lift wet paint from the paper. This works well for creating soft highlights or adjusting the intensity of a wash. For more precise lifting, you can use a small, stiff brush or even the tip of a paper towel. When working with dried paint, you may need to rewet the area slightly before attempting to lift the color.

Another effective lifting technique is to use a lifting preparation, which is a liquid that helps to soften dried watercolor paint, making it easier to remove. Apply the preparation to the area you want to lift, allow it to sit for a few moments, then gently blot or scrub the area with a clean brush or paper towel. This method can be particularly useful for creating highlights in areas of dark pigment or for correcting mistakes.

It's important to note that lifting techniques work best on paper that is specifically designed for watercolor painting. Cheaper papers may not hold up well to repeated lifting and scrubbing, so invest in high-quality watercolor paper for best results.

## Using Masking Fluid and Other Resist Methods

Masking fluid, also known as liquid frisket, is a valuable tool in the watercolor artist's arsenal. This liquid latex solution is applied to areas of the paper that you want to protect from paint. Once dry, you can paint freely over the masked areas, and when the masking fluid is removed, it reveals pristine white paper beneath.

Using masking fluid requires some practice and patience, but it can yield stunning results. To begin, make sure your paper is completely dry before applying the masking fluid. Use a dedicated brush or a masking fluid pen to apply the solution precisely where you want it. Allow the masking fluid to dry completely before painting over it.

When you're ready to remove the masking fluid, gently rub it with a clean eraser or your fingertip. Be careful not to damage the paper surface as you remove the mask. Once the masking fluid is removed, you'll be left with crisp, white shapes that you can then paint into or leave as highlights in your composition.

Masking fluid is particularly useful for preserving small, intricate details in your painting, such as the pistils of flowers, the whiskers on an animal's face, or the rigging on a sailboat. It's also an excellent tool for creating texture effects, such as the spray of a waterfall or the sparkle of sunlight on water.

While masking fluid is perhaps the most well-known resist method, there are other techniques you can explore as well. Wax resist, for example, involves drawing on your paper with a white wax crayon before applying watercolor washes. The wax repels the paint, creating interesting textures and patterns.

Another resist method is salt resist, where you sprinkle salt onto wet watercolor paint. As the paint dries, the salt absorbs some of the pigment, creating a mottled, textured effect. This technique can be particularly effective for creating the appearance of rough stone, sand, or foliage.

Experiment with different resist methods to discover which ones work best for your painting style and subject matter. Remember that these techniques often require some trial and error, so don't be discouraged if your first attempts don't turn out exactly as you envisioned. With practice, you'll develop a feel for how to incorporate these resist methods into your work effectively.

### Incorporating Mixed Media Elements

While watercolor is a beautiful medium on its own, combining it with other materials can lead to exciting and innovative results. Mixed media techniques can add texture, depth, and visual interest to your watercolor paintings, pushing the boundaries of what's possible with this versatile medium.

One popular mixed media approach is to combine watercolor with ink. You might start with a loose watercolor underpainting and then add crisp, detailed linework with ink pens or brushes. This technique can be particularly effective for architectural subjects or botanical illustrations, where you want to combine the softness of watercolor washes with precise, detailed lines.

Another interesting combination is watercolor with colored pencils. Use watercolor to establish your basic shapes and color scheme, then add details and texture with colored pencils once the paint is dry. This technique allows you to achieve a level of detail that can be challenging with watercolor alone, while still maintaining the luminous quality of the paint.

Collage is another mixed media technique that can work beautifully with watercolor. Try incorporating torn paper, fabric scraps, or even natural materials like leaves or flower petals into your watercolor paintings. These elements can add interesting textures and create a sense of depth in your work.

For those interested in more experimental approaches, consider incorporating water-soluble media like watercolor crayons or water-soluble graphite into your paintings. These materials can be applied dry and then activated with water, creating interesting effects and textures that blend seamlessly with traditional watercolor techniques.

When working with mixed media, it's important to consider the compatibility of your materials. Some mediums may not adhere well to watercolor paper, or may interact unexpectedly with your paints. Always test your combinations on a scrap piece of paper before incorporating them into a finished piece.

It's also crucial to think about the archival quality of your mixed media work. Some materials may fade or deteriorate over time, so if longevity is a concern, be sure to use high-quality, archival-grade materials throughout your piece.

As you explore mixed media techniques, remember that the goal is to enhance your watercolor painting, not to overpower it. Use these additional elements judiciously, always keeping in mind how they contribute to your overall composition and artistic vision.

Incorporating advanced techniques like negative painting, lifting, masking, and mixed media into your watercolor practice can open up new realms of creative possibility. These methods allow you to achieve effects that go beyond traditional watercolor techniques, adding depth, texture, and complexity to your work.

As you continue to develop your skills, you'll find that these advanced techniques become valuable tools in your artistic repertoire. They'll allow you to tackle more complex subjects, express your ideas more fully, and develop a unique artistic voice. Remember that mastering these techniques takes time and practice, so be patient with yourself as you experiment and learn.

In the next chapter, we'll explore how to take all the skills and techniques you've learned throughout this book and use them to develop your personal style as a watercolor artist. We'll discuss finding inspiration, experimenting with different approaches, and developing a practice routine that will help you continue to grow and evolve as an artist.

# Chapter 10: Developing Your Personal Style

As we near the conclusion of our journey through the art of watercolor, it's time to explore the most exciting and personal aspect of your artistic development: finding your unique style. In the previous chapter, we delved into advanced techniques that push the boundaries of traditional watercolor painting. Now, we'll focus on how to harness these skills, along with your own experiences and inspirations, to create a body of work that is distinctly yours.

## Finding inspiration and subject matter

The quest for inspiration is a lifelong journey for any artist. It's a deeply personal process that evolves as you grow and change. For some, inspiration might strike suddenly, like a bolt of lightning, while for others, it's a slow burn that develops over time. Regardless of how it manifests, cultivating a keen eye for potential subject matter is crucial in developing your personal style.

One of the most effective ways to find inspiration is to immerse yourself in the world around you. Take long walks in nature, explore urban landscapes, or people-watch in busy cafes. The renowned watercolor artist Joseph Zbukvic once said, "The world is full of paintings waiting to be painted." This sentiment encapsulates the idea that inspiration can be found anywhere if you're open to seeing it.

Keep a sketchbook with you at all times. This practice, advocated by countless artists throughout history, allows you to capture fleeting moments of inspiration. Quick sketches, color notes, and even written descriptions can serve as valuable references for future paintings. The act of sketching itself can also help train your eye to see the world in terms of composition, color, and form.

Travel can be an incredible source of inspiration. Experiencing new cultures, landscapes, and ways of life can broaden your perspective and infuse your work with fresh energy. The famous watercolorist John Singer Sargent produced some of his most vibrant and expressive work during his travels through Europe and the Middle East. Even if you can't travel far, exploring your local area with fresh eyes can yield surprising results.

Literature, music, and other forms of art can also spark inspiration. Reading poetry might inspire you to capture the mood or imagery described in words through your watercolors. Listening to music could influence the rhythm and flow of your brushstrokes. Studying the work of other visual artists, not just watercolorists, can expose you to new ideas about color, composition, and subject matter.

Personal experiences and emotions are perhaps the most powerful sources of inspiration. Your unique life story, memories, and feelings can inform your work in ways that make it truly individual. The abstract expressionist Helen Frankenthaler, who began her career working in watercolor, once said, "There are no rules. That is how art is born, how breakthroughs happen. Go against the rules or ignore the rules. That is what invention is about."

As you explore different sources of inspiration, you may find yourself drawn to certain themes or subjects. This natural gravitation is often the first step in developing a personal style. Perhaps you're consistently captivated by the play of light on water, or you find yourself repeatedly painting scenes from your childhood. Embrace these recurring themes; they are the threads that will weave together to form the tapestry of your artistic voice.

However, it's important to strike a balance between focusing on subjects that resonate with you and challenging yourself with new subject matter. Stepping out of your comfort zone can lead to exciting discoveries and prevent your work from becoming stagnant. If you typically paint landscapes, try your hand at portraiture. If you're comfortable with realistic depictions, experiment with abstraction.

The subject matter you choose to focus on can also be influenced by the unique qualities of watercolor as a medium. The transparency and fluidity of watercolor lend themselves beautifully to certain subjects. Misty landscapes, delicate flowers, and shimmering reflections on water are all subjects that watercolor can capture with unparalleled beauty. As you develop your style, you may find that you're particularly drawn to subjects that showcase the strengths of the medium.

Remember that inspiration is not just about what you paint, but also about why you paint it. What stories do you want to tell through your art? What emotions do you want to evoke in your viewers? What aspects of the world do you want to highlight or explore? Answering these questions can help guide your choice of subject matter and infuse your work with deeper meaning.

## Experimenting with different styles and approaches

Once you've identified sources of inspiration and subject matter that resonate with you, the next step in developing your personal style is to experiment with different approaches to watercolor painting. This experimentation phase is crucial; it's where you'll discover the techniques, color palettes, and compositional strategies that feel most natural and expressive to you.

Start by studying the work of watercolor masters, both historical and contemporary. Analyze their use of color, brushwork, and composition. Try to recreate some of their paintings as studies. This exercise isn't about copying, but about understanding the choices these artists made and how those choices contribute to their unique styles. You might find yourself drawn to the loose, expressive style of artists like Emil Carlsen, or the precise, detailed approach of botanical artists like Maria Sibylla Merian.

As you explore different styles, pay attention to how they make you feel. Which approaches excite you? Which ones feel uncomfortable or forced? Your emotional response to different styles can be a valuable guide in developing your own. The influential art educator and artist Robert Henri once said, "Don't worry about your originality. You couldn't get rid of it even if you wanted to. It will stick with you and show up for better or worse in spite of all you or anyone else can do."

Experiment with different levels of abstraction and realism. Some artists find their voice in hyper-realistic depictions of their subjects, while others prefer to distill their subjects down to their essential forms and colors. Try both extremes and everything in between. You might discover that your personal style lies somewhere in the middle, combining elements of realism with more abstract or expressive elements.

Color is another area ripe for experimentation. Try working with limited color palettes, using only two or three colors in a painting. Then, go to the other extreme and use every color in your palette. Experiment with harmonious color schemes and bold, contrasting ones. The way you use color can become a defining characteristic of your style. The artist Wolf Kahn, known for his vibrant landscapes, once said, "I use color to describe space and shape."

Brushwork is yet another aspect of watercolor painting where you can develop a distinctive approach. Experiment with different brush sizes and shapes. Try using unconventional tools like sponges, credit cards, or even your fingers to apply paint. Some artists develop a style characterized by bold, confident brushstrokes, while others prefer a more delicate, precise approach. Your unique way of handling the brush can become a signature element of your style.

Don't be afraid to combine watercolor with other media. Many contemporary artists are pushing the boundaries of traditional watercolor by incorporating elements of collage, ink, or even digital media into their work. This mixed-media approach can lead to exciting new possibilities and help you carve out a unique niche in the art world.

As you experiment, keep a record of your attempts. This could be in the form of a sketchbook, a digital portfolio, or simply by keeping all your paintings, successful or not. Looking back on this body of work can help you identify patterns and preferences that are emerging in your style.

Remember that developing a personal style is not about forcing yourself to paint in a certain way. It's about discovering the approaches that feel most authentic and expressive to you. As the artist Georgia O'Keeffe wisely stated, "I have already settled it for myself so flattery and criticism go down the same drain and I am quite free."

# Chapter 14: Preserving and Presenting Your Work

As we near the conclusion of our journey through the art of watercolor painting, it's essential to consider how to protect and showcase the fruits of your labor. The delicate nature of watercolor paintings requires special care to ensure their longevity and preserve their beauty for years to come. In this chapter, we'll explore the various aspects of preserving and presenting your watercolor artwork, from proper storage and framing techniques to digitizing your paintings and exhibiting your art.

## Proper storage and framing

The first step in preserving your watercolor paintings is to ensure they are stored correctly when not on display. Watercolor paintings are particularly sensitive to environmental factors such as light, humidity, and temperature fluctuations. To protect your artwork, it's crucial to store them in a cool, dry place away from direct sunlight. Many artists choose to keep their paintings in acid-free archival boxes or portfolios, which provide an additional layer of protection against dust and physical damage.

When it comes to framing your watercolor paintings, the choices you make can significantly impact both the preservation and presentation of your work. The primary purpose of framing is not just to enhance the aesthetic appeal of your painting but also to protect it from environmental factors that could cause deterioration over time. One of the most important considerations when framing watercolors is the use of acid-free materials. Acid-free mats and backing boards help prevent the yellowing and degradation of your paper over time.

Glass is another crucial component of framing watercolors. While regular glass can protect your painting from dust and physical damage, it does not offer protection against harmful UV rays, which can cause fading and discoloration of your pigments over time. For this reason, many artists and collectors opt for UV-protective glass or acrylic glazing. These materials filter out a significant portion of UV light, helping to preserve the vibrancy of your colors for decades.

When mounting your watercolor painting, it's essential to use archival-quality hinges or corners. These should be made from acid-free materials and should allow for some movement of the paper as it expands and contracts with changes in humidity. Avoid using adhesives directly on the back of your painting, as these can cause discoloration and damage over time.

The choice of frame itself is largely a matter of personal preference and should complement the style of your painting. However, it's important to ensure that the frame is sturdy enough to protect your artwork and that it allows for proper air circulation to prevent the buildup of moisture between the painting and the glass.

Renowned watercolor artist Joseph Zbukvic emphasizes the importance of proper framing: "A good frame is like a stage for your painting. It should enhance the work without overshadowing it. But more than that, it's a protective shell that, when done right, can help your watercolor last for generations."

## Digitizing your watercolor paintings

In today's digital age, digitizing your watercolor paintings has become an increasingly important aspect of preserving and sharing your work. High-quality digital reproductions of your paintings can serve multiple purposes, from creating prints and merchandise to sharing your work online or submitting it for juried exhibitions.

The process of digitizing watercolor paintings requires careful attention to detail to ensure that the digital version accurately represents the original work. The first step is to capture a high-resolution image of your painting. This can be done using a high-quality digital camera or a professional scanner designed for artwork. When using a camera, it's crucial to pay attention to lighting conditions. Natural, diffused light often produces the best results, as it helps to accurately capture the subtle hues and tones of your watercolor painting.

If you're using a scanner, make sure it's large enough to accommodate your artwork. Many artists prefer flatbed scanners for their ability to capture fine details and textures. When scanning, use the highest resolution possible, typically 300 dpi or higher for print-quality reproductions.

Once you have captured your digital image, the next step is to process and color-correct it to match the original as closely as possible. This can be done using photo editing software such as Adobe Photoshop or GIMP. Pay particular attention to the color balance, contrast, and sharpness of the image. It's often helpful to have the original painting on hand for comparison during this process.

Digital artist and watercolor enthusiast James Gurney advises, "When digitizing your watercolors, remember that the goal is not to improve or alter the original, but to create the most faithful digital representation possible. This requires patience and a good eye for color and detail."

Once you have a high-quality digital version of your painting, you can use it for various purposes. You can create limited edition prints, use the image on your website or social media platforms, or include it in your digital portfolio. Having digital versions of your work also provides a form of backup, preserving a record of your painting even if something were to happen to the original.

## Exhibiting and selling your art

Exhibiting your watercolor paintings is a crucial step in sharing your art with the world and potentially launching a career as a professional artist. There are numerous venues and opportunities for exhibiting watercolor paintings, ranging from local art fairs and galleries to national and international watercolor societies.

One of the first steps in exhibiting your work is to build a cohesive body of work. This doesn't mean that all your paintings need to look the same, but there should be a consistent level of quality and a recognizable style or theme running through your collection. Many galleries and exhibitions look for artists who have developed a unique voice or perspective in their work.

When preparing for an exhibition, pay close attention to the presentation of your work. This includes not only the framing, which we discussed earlier, but also how you arrange and display your paintings. Consider the flow and narrative of your exhibition. How do your paintings relate to each other? Is there a story or theme that emerges when they're viewed together?

Creating an artist statement is another important aspect of exhibiting your work. This short text should provide insight into your artistic process, inspirations, and the themes you explore in your work. It helps viewers connect with your art on a deeper level and can be a valuable tool for marketing your work to galleries and collectors.

Pricing your artwork can be one of the most challenging aspects of selling your watercolor paintings. It's important to consider factors such as the size of the painting, the time and materials invested, your reputation as an artist, and the local market for watercolor art. Don't be afraid to ask for advice from more experienced artists or gallery owners.

Watercolor artist Mary Whyte shares her perspective on exhibiting: "Exhibiting your work is not just about selling paintings. It's about engaging with your audience, learning from their reactions, and growing as an artist. Every exhibition is an opportunity to see your work through fresh eyes."

In addition to traditional exhibitions, many artists are finding success in selling their work online. Platforms like Etsy, Saatchi Art, and personal websites provide opportunities to reach a global audience. When selling online, high-quality images of your work are crucial, which is where your digitization skills come into play.

Social media platforms like Instagram and Facebook can also be powerful tools for promoting your work and connecting with potential buyers and galleries. Regular posts showcasing your paintings, works in progress, and insights into your artistic process can help build a following and create opportunities for sales and exhibitions.

Remember that selling your art is as much about building relationships as it is about the quality of your work. Networking with other artists, gallery owners, and collectors can open doors to new opportunities. Attend art openings, join local art associations, and participate in workshops and painting events to expand your network within the art community.

As we conclude this chapter on preserving and presenting your work, it's important to remember that these skills are an integral part of your journey as a watercolor artist. Proper care and presentation of your paintings ensure that your creative efforts are protected and can be enjoyed for years to come. Digitizing your work opens up new possibilities for sharing and selling your art, while exhibiting provides opportunities for growth, recognition, and connection with your audience.

In the next and final chapter, we'll explore how to develop your personal style as a watercolor artist, bringing together all the skills and techniques we've discussed throughout this book to help you find your unique voice in the world of watercolor painting.

## Tips for continuous improvement and practice

Developing your personal style is not a destination, but a journey that continues throughout your artistic career. Even after you've found a style that feels authentically yours, there's always room for growth and refinement. Here are some strategies to ensure continuous improvement in your watercolor practice.

Establish a regular painting routine. Consistency is key in developing and maintaining your skills. Set aside dedicated time for your art, even if it's just a few hours a week. Many successful artists swear by the practice of painting every day, even if it's just a quick sketch. The watercolor master Charles Reid advised, "Paint something every day, even if it's just for 15 minutes."

Challenge yourself with new subjects and techniques. Once you've found a comfortable style, it can be tempting to stick with what works. However, pushing yourself out of your comfort zone is essential for growth. If you typically paint landscapes, try your hand at portraiture. If you usually work in a loose, expressive style, experiment with more detailed, precise work. These challenges can help you discover new aspects of your style and prevent your work from becoming formulaic.

Seek constructive criticism. While it's important to trust your own artistic instincts, feedback from others can provide valuable insights. Join a local art group, take classes, or participate in online art communities where you can share your work and receive critiques. Be open to feedback, but also learn to filter it. Not all advice will align with your artistic vision, and that's okay. The key is to consider different perspectives while staying true to your own voice.

Study the work of other artists, both historical and contemporary. Analyze how they handle color, composition, and technique. Visit art galleries and museums whenever possible to see original works in person. The artist John Salminen emphasizes the importance of this practice: "I think it's critical to study the masters... not to copy them, but to understand how they think."

Experiment with different materials and surfaces. Try new brands of paint, paper, or brushes. Each material has its own characteristics that can influence your painting process and the final result. You might discover that a particular combination of materials allows you to express your style more effectively.

Keep a sketchbook or journal. Use it to jot down ideas, make quick sketches, and record your thoughts about your artistic process. This practice can help you track your progress, identify recurring themes in your work, and spark new ideas for paintings.

Participate in art challenges or competitions. These can provide structure to your practice and motivate you to create work on a deadline. They can also expose your work to a wider audience and potentially lead to new opportunities.

Consider taking workshops or classes, even if you're an experienced artist. Learning from other skilled painters can expose you to new techniques and perspectives. The watercolor artist Alvaro Castagnet advises, "Never stop learning. Art is a lifetime journey."

Practice mindfulness in your painting process. Pay attention to your thoughts and feelings as you work. Are you enjoying the process? Are you feeling frustrated? This self-awareness can help you identify which aspects of painting bring you the most satisfaction and guide you towards a style that feels authentically yours.

Finally, remember that developing your personal style is not about achieving perfection. It's about expressing your unique vision and continually growing as an artist. Embrace the journey, with all its challenges and discoveries. As the artist Robert Genn once said, "The job of the artist is always to deepen the mystery."

As we conclude this chapter and our exploration of watercolor painting, remember that the skills and techniques we've discussed throughout this book are tools to help you express your unique artistic vision. Your personal style will emerge naturally as you paint more, experiment fearlessly, and stay true to your artistic instincts. Trust in your journey, and let your love for watercolor guide you towards creating art that is truly your own.


As we conclude our journey through "The Art of Watercolor Made Easy," we hope you've discovered the beauty and versatility of this captivating medium. From its rich history to the myriad techniques explored, watercolor painting offers endless possibilities for artistic expression. We've delved into the fundamentals of color theory, essential techniques, and the importance of transparency in creating luminous works of art.

Throughout this book, we've explored various subjects, from expansive landscapes to intimate portraits, each presenting unique challenges and opportunities for growth. The principles of composition and design have been emphasized, providing you with the tools to create balanced and visually striking paintings. We've also examined advanced techniques and mixed media approaches, encouraging you to push the boundaries of traditional watercolor painting.

Perhaps most importantly, we've emphasized the development of your personal style. By experimenting with different approaches and finding inspiration in the world around you, you can cultivate a unique artistic voice. Remember that mastery of watercolor is a lifelong journey, one that requires patience, practice, and a willingness to embrace both successes and failures as learning opportunities.

As you continue your watercolor adventure, we encourage you to approach each painting with curiosity and enthusiasm. Allow yourself to be inspired by the transparency and fluidity of the medium, and don't be afraid to take risks and explore new techniques. With dedication and perseverance, you'll find that the challenges of watercolor painting become opportunities for growth and self-expression.

In the end, the true beauty of watercolor lies not just in the finished painting, but in the process itself. Embrace the unpredictability of the medium, learn to work with water rather than against it, and find joy in the moment of creation. As you apply the techniques and principles outlined in this book, remember that your unique perspective and experiences will bring life to your artwork in ways that no one else can replicate.

May your watercolor journey be filled with discovery, growth, and the sheer pleasure of bringing your vision to life on paper. Happy painting!